HER Business Planner (

Especially designed to help you to overcome barriers in your business journey & support you in surviving a crisis.

Serena Fordham

Special thanks to all of the HER Business Revolution Superwomen Membership Club members who I have supported and coached, & who have inspired this planner & journal to help other amazing Female Entrepreneurs & Business Boss Women!

PART 1: BUSINESS PLANNING

When faced with any barriers to business, or a bigger life crisis, it is important to stop, reflect and plan in order to move forwards successfully and sustainably.

Reflecting When Faced With Barriers/Crisis

When reflecting HER Business Revolution recommends completing a SWOT Analysis to identify the current situation of your business.

Strengths:

- What are your strengths?
- How can you best promote them?

Weaknesses:

- What are your weaknesses?
- How can you overcome these?
- What are your contingency plans for if the worst happens?

Opportunities:

- Can you look "outside of the box" and offer something different?
- Can you offer something for free/low cost/in exchange for something else of value to you?

- What is demanded now?
- What ways can you meet this demand?

Threats:

- What affects your business and industry negatively?
- How can you safeguard against them?
- What ways can remove them all together?

Planning When Faced With Barriers/Crisis

When planning HER Business Revolution recommends to do the following:

1. Make one list of what you can control and one list of what you can't control.

2. Rip up/burn/throw away (in a ritual-like fashion) your "can't control" list.

3. On your "can control" list identify the things you can continue to do the same (that are unaffected by the barrier/crisis) and highlight those things that you can't keep the same.

4. Focusing on your highlighted things, think of/ask for ways you could do the things differently/diversify/be creative to move these parts of business forwards in the crisis - e.g. create a lower cost option, change it to cater for a wider or different target audience, adapt it to suit current problems and provide solutions to them.

5. Prioritise your whole list from the things you can do quickly to make money, to the things that will take most time to change/adapt to make money - note: your unchanged business activities will likely be at the top of your list!

If you try this exercise and get stuck at any point, just reach out for support...

- Who can you ask for help?
- What can you offer them in return?
- What resources and strengths do they have to add value?

"Out of the Box" Thinking

We talked previously about "out of the box" thinking, so to encourage you to think about these, here are practical examples of what we mean by this.

1. Look at delivering offline activities online...E.g. Therapy sessions, craft workshops, fitness workouts online through Zoom, Skype, etc.

2. Look at ways of offering your product/service at a lower cost price point to overcome price objections...E.g. A course, workbook, book, activity pack, etc.

3. Look at alternative work or passive income opportunities (but don't feel pressured to just grab at anything in desperation, including joining a MLM or going back into employment!)...E.g. Collaborate with others in your industry to offer something amazing at a lower cost and attract more people, reach out to businesses who seem to be thriving and offer your services/support/expertise, or look at investing or using what money you do have to create diverse opportunities, etc.

Setting Your Goals

"A Goal Without a Plan is Just a Wish."

Goal setting is a fundamental part of growth and the reason behind consistent results - and is especially important when faced with any kind of barrier or crisis.

Your goals are to be loyally protected and freed from any distractions which may come in to play on your journey. Distractions (that are even more present and heightened during a crisis) come into play due to the noisy world which we all live in, but they only tend to take over when you do not plan and set your goals properly.

Success does not happen by accident – it takes determination, courage, specific goals (plus complete value placed on these goals) in order to keep the fire inside of you burning when distractions or barriers appear.

The Difference Between a Goal and Your Vision

Your vision is your end result, it's how you vision your business and life to look like 12 months from now, 3 years from now, 5 years, 10 years, etc.

Your goals are your visions broken down - think of your goals as stepping stones to get to your vision. You can't just leap straight from where you are now into your long-term vision, you have to break it down and achieve the small goals each month in order to be rewarded with your long term wants.

This starts by getting crystal clear on your vision, where you want to be in 12 months, 3 years, 5 years, 10 years, etc, and then breaking that down by setting your goals each month.

It's important to remember that your visions and goals are fuelled by your desires — so keep in tune with this when connecting and visualising these. If you have difficulty, give yourself compassion and redirect your train of thought back to your desired results.

How Do I Connect With my Vision?

There are some who connect with their visualisations without their minds straying, whilst some report to struggle with this.

When connecting with your vision it's really important to remember self-love, and to allow your mind to be redirected back to the connection of your vision without any judgement.

With practice, this becomes easier and much more enjoyable.

To help with this exercise, take half an hour of quietness with no distractions to brainstorm everything you would like from your life. Remember - do not limit yourself, really go for what you want and get it all out on paper!

After this you can begin the process of 'A day in the life...' This involves placing yourself in the picture of exactly what your day looks like 1 year, 3 years, 5 years, 10 years, etc from now. When doing this, be sure to really go into detail and not to hold back, and be as creative as you possibly can be, as this will really help you to fully connect with your vision.

Some find it easier to create a vision board to really connect with their vision. This is your opportunity to get creative and colourful, by finding pictures associated with what you want for your life and business, and attaching these to your vision board and putting this up somewhere so you can be reminded of your vision every single day.

How do I Become Clear on How my Goals Will be Achieved?

Start by brainstorming all of the things you need to do/actions you need to take to achieve your goal.

Now put these all in order and write them in the steps to goal section within the HER Back to Basics Business Planner below, with the date you are going to achieve them by.

Start Brainstorming Here…

HER Back to Basics Business Planner

Why did I start out on your business journey?

_____

_____

_____

The service/product which I am bringing to other people's lives is…

_____

_____

_____

My product/service is amazing because it will…

1._____

2._____

3._____

4._____

5. _____

My 'WHY' is...

_____

_____

_____

My 'Perfect Client' will gain and achieve whilst working with me by...

_____

_____

_____

My 'Perfect Clients' Pains are…

_____

_____

_____

_____

_____

_____

My 'Perfect Clients' Vision and Happy Place is…

_____

_____

If I was to place myself within my 'Perfect Clients'
Shoes, the content I would need right now would be…

_____

_____

I currently FEEL 'stuck' with...

_____

_____

_____

I can 'unstick' myself by...

_____

_____

_____

My visions for my business and life are...

Year 1._____

Year 3._____

Year 5._____

Year 10. _____

This month's goal which I WILL hit towards my Year 1 vision is...

_____

_____

_____

Pick the most important goal, your primary goal, little or big.

The steps I need to take in order to reach my goal are...

_____

_____

_____

_____

_____

_____

Whilst claiming my goal, my self-care plan will be…

_____

_____

_____

_____

_____

_____

Repeat the above few steps for other monthly goals as appropriate.

Using Planners for Focus

Using the HER Focused Weekly Planner and HER Revolutionary Daily Planner to plan your days keeps you focused on the actions you need to take to achieve your goals.

When completing your planners it is important to use motivating phrases in order to shift any blocks around motivation when hitting your goals.

By being aware of your language and changing it where needed, and using words which keep you attached to your desire and encourage you to remember your WHY, this means that you are more likely to feel positive towards completing the actions to achieve your goals.

Some examples include...

- 'Going to the gym' - 'I'm getting my sexy back'
- 'Family time' - 'Bonding time with my babies'
- 'Morning Routine' - 'Awakening my genius'
- 'Work time' - 'Doing my due to feed my family'
- 'Sideline income' - 'Shaping my destiny'
- 'Me time' - 'self-love time'

And remember…

"The flower does not dream of the bee and the bee comes!"

HER Focused
Weekly Planner

mon.

tues.

wed.

thurs.

fri.

sat.

sun.

HER Focused
Weekly Planner

mon.

tues.

wed.

thurs.

fri.

sat.

sun.

HER Focused
Weekly Planner

mon.

tues.

wed.

thurs.

fri.

sat.

sun.

HER Focused
Weekly Planner

mon.

tues.

wed.

thurs.

fri.

sat.

sun.

HER Focused
Weekly Planner

mon.

tues.

wed.

thurs.

fri.

sat.

sun.

HER Focused
Weekly Planner

mon.

tues.

wed.

thurs.

fri.

sat.

sun.

HER Focused
Weekly Planner

mon.

tues.

wed.

thurs.

fri.

sat.

sun.

HER Focused
Weekly Planner

mon.

tues.

wed.

thurs.

fri.

sat.

sun.

HER Focused
Weekly Planner

mon.

tues.

wed.

thurs.

fri.

sat.

sun.

HER Focused
Weekly Planner

mon.

tues.

wed.

thurs.

fri.

sat.

sun.

HER Revolutionary Daily Planner

HER Business Revolution
Because we are all superwomen

DATE: ....

IMPORTANT TASKS

HEALTHY EATING

EXERCISE

CLOSER TO YOUR GOAL

MORNING

AFTERNOON

EVENING

WATER

DATE: ....

IMPORTANT TASKS

MORNING

HEALTHY EATING

....
....
....
....

AFTERNOON

EXERCISE

☆ ....
☆ ....
☆ ....

EVENING

CLOSER TO YOUR GOAL

☆ ....

WATER ⊔⊔⊔⊔⊔⊔⊔

☆ ....

HER Revolutionary Daily Planner

DATE: ....

IMPORTANT TASKS

-
-
-
-
-

HEALTHY EATING

....

....

....

....

EXERCISE

⭐ ....

⭐ ....

⭐ ....

CLOSER TO YOUR GOAL

⭐ ....

MORNING

AFTERNOON

EVENING

WATER ⬜⬜⬜⬜⬜⬜⬜

⭐ ....

HER Revolutionary Daily Planner

DATE: ....

IMPORTANT TASKS

MORNING

AFTERNOON

HEALTHY EATING

....
....
....
....

EVENING

EXERCISE

....
....
....

CLOSER TO YOUR GOAL

....

WATER

....

33

HER
Business
Revolution

Because we are all superwomen

DATE: ....

IMPORTANT TASKS

MORNING

HEALTHY EATING

....
....
....
....

AFTERNOON

EXERCISE

....
....
....

EVENING

CLOSER TO YOUR GOAL

....

WATER

....

HER Revolutionary Daily Planner

DATE: ....

IMPORTANT TASKS

MORNING

AFTERNOON

EVENING

HEALTHY EATING

EXERCISE

CLOSER TO YOUR GOAL

WATER

HER
Business
Revolution

Because we are all superwomen

DATE: ....

IMPORTANT TASKS

MORNING

HEALTHY EATING

AFTERNOON

EXERCISE

⭐
⭐
⭐

EVENING

CLOSER TO YOUR GOAL

⭐

WATER ⊔⊔⊔⊔⊔⊔⊔

⭐

HER Revolutionary Daily Planner

DATE: ....

IMPORTANT TASKS

MORNING

AFTERNOON

HEALTHY EATING

EVENING

EXERCISE

CLOSER TO YOUR GOAL

WATER

HER Revolutionary Daily Planner

DATE: ....

IMPORTANT TASKS

MORNING

HEALTHY EATING

....
....
....
....

AFTERNOON

EXERCISE

⭐ ....
⭐ ....
⭐ ....

EVENING

CLOSER TO YOUR GOAL

⭐ ....

WATER ▢▢▢▢▢▢▢

⭐ ....

HER Revolutionary Daily Planner

DATE: ....

IMPORTANT TASKS

MORNING

AFTERNOON

EVENING

HEALTHY EATING

....
....
....
....

EXERCISE

....
....
....

CLOSER TO YOUR GOAL

....

WATER

....

HER Revolutionary Daily Planner

DATE: ....

IMPORTANT TASKS

HEALTHY EATING

EXERCISE

CLOSER TO YOUR GOAL

MORNING

AFTERNOON

EVENING

WATER

HER Revolutionary Daily Planner

DATE: ....

IMPORTANT TASKS

MORNING

AFTERNOON

HEALTHY EATING

....
....
....
....

EVENING

EXERCISE

CLOSER TO YOUR GOAL

WATER

HER Revolutionary Daily Planner

HER Business Revolution
Because we are all superwomen

DATE: ....

MORNING

IMPORTANT TASKS

HEALTHY EATING

AFTERNOON

EXERCISE

⭐
⭐
⭐

EVENING

CLOSER TO YOUR GOAL

⭐ ....

WATER

⭐ ....

HER Revolutionary Daily Planner

DATE: ....

IMPORTANT TASKS

MORNING

AFTERNOON

HEALTHY EATING

....
....
....
....

EVENING

EXERCISE

CLOSER TO YOUR GOAL

WATER

HER Business Revolution

Because we are all superwomen

DATE: ....

IMPORTANT TASKS

MORNING

AFTERNOON

EVENING

HEALTHY EATING

EXERCISE

CLOSER TO YOUR GOAL

WATER

HER Revolutionary Daily Planner

DATE: ....

IMPORTANT TASKS

MORNING

AFTERNOON

HEALTHY EATING

....
....
....
....

EVENING

EXERCISE

....
....
....

CLOSER TO YOUR GOAL

....

WATER

....

HER Revolutionary Daily Planner

HER Business Revolution
Because we are all superwomen

DATE: ....

IMPORTANT TASKS

MORNING

AFTERNOON

HEALTHY EATING

EVENING

EXERCISE

CLOSER TO YOUR GOAL

WATER

HER Revolutionary Daily Planner

DATE: ....

IMPORTANT TASKS

MORNING

HEALTHY EATING

....
....
....
....

AFTERNOON

EXERCISE

⭐ ....
⭐ ....
⭐ ....

EVENING

CLOSER TO YOUR GOAL

⭐ ....

WATER 🥛🥛🥛🥛🥛🥛🥛

⭐ ....

HER Revolutionary Daily Planner

DATE: ....

IMPORTANT TASKS

HEALTHY EATING

EXERCISE

CLOSER TO YOUR GOAL

MORNING

AFTERNOON

EVENING

WATER

DATE: ....

IMPORTANT TASKS

MORNING

AFTERNOON

HEALTHY EATING

EVENING

EXERCISE

CLOSER TO YOUR GOAL

WATER

PART 2: WELLBEING JOURNAL

Your mental health and wellbeing can suffer a lot when you are faced with barriers (or a crisis), therefore it is important that you focus on improving these so you are in the best possible shape (in terms of health and mindset) to be able to move your business forwards during challenging times.

Mindset When Faced With Barriers/Crisis

Mindset plays a huge part in how well you will overcome any barriers (or crisis points) throughout your business journey.

You might experience thoughts like…

- "No one wants to buy my stuff at this time."
- "I can't possibly do that."
- "Me and my business aren't good enough."
- Etc.

However, all these negative thoughts do is put extra blocks and barriers in your way to making sales and money within your business, and will stop you from achieving your goals, and thus your overall vision.

It is important to remember that us business women come across situations, negativity and barriers constantly throughout their business journey, and any time of crisis is no different. So, when you come to a hurdle, just find a creative, innovative and effective way to jump over it, go under it, or scooch around it in order for your business to develop, thrive and grow moving forwards.

Positive Daily Affirmations

Some prefer to use meditation, music or other mindfulness practices, however starting each day with some affirmations can really help to set you up for a positive and productive day ahead.

Here are some examples you can use…

- I deeply and completely love myself, trust myself, honour myself, and accept myself for who I am.
- I create my own safety and security easily.
- I always take care of my own needs first.
- I am worthy of the best that life has to offer me.
- I am worthy of amazing feedback and beautiful compliments that touch me and feed my soul.
- I am worthy of making my purpose my reality.
- I am allowed to be wrong – mistakes are life's lessons.
- I may not know everything, but I am always learning and growing.
- I am free to be who I want to be, with no judgements.
- I have the freedom to choose my own destiny, and there are no restrictions.
- I am worthy of being seen and heard.
- I am worthy of speaking my truth and being understood.
- I am important in this world.

- I am totally in love with my life.
- I have everything I need and want in my life.
- I am grateful for all the opportunities I have available to me.
- My life is amazing, and I have got here because of me.
- I welcome abundance easily.
- My earning potential and wealth abundance is limitless.
- My confidence is soaring.
- I am in control of my life and how I react to the world around me.
- I have the power to make the world a better place.
- I am brave and beautiful.
- I am kind and loyal.
- I am ambitious and passionate.
- I am blessed and loved.

HER Daily
Affirmations

mon. I am...

tues. I am...

wed. I am...

thurs. I am...

fri. I am...

sat. I am...

sun. I am...

HER Daily
Affirmations

mon. I am...

tues. I am...

wed. I am...

thurs. I am...

fri. I am...

sat. I am...

sun. I am...

HER Daily Affirmations

mon. I am...

tues. I am...

wed. I am...

thurs. I am...

fri. I am...

sat. I am...

sun. I am...

HER Daily
Affirmations

mon. I am...

tues. I am...

wed. I am...

thurs. I am...

fri. I am...

sat. I am...

sun. I am...

HER Daily Affirmations

mon. I am...

tues. I am...

wed. I am...

thurs. I am...

fri. I am...

sat. I am...

sun. I am...

HER Daily
Affirmations

mon. I am...

tues. I am...

wed. I am...

thurs. I am...

fri. I am...

sat. I am...

sun. I am...

HER Daily
Affirmations

mon. I am...

tues. I am...

wed. I am...

thurs. I am...

fri. I am...

sat. I am...

sun. I am...

HER Daily
Affirmations

mon. I am...

tues. I am...

wed. I am...

thurs. I am...

fri. I am...

sat. I am...

sun. I am...

HER Daily
Affirmations

mon. I am...

tues. I am...

wed. I am...

thurs. I am...

fri. I am...

sat. I am...

sun. I am...

HER Daily
Affirmations

mon. I am...

tues. I am...

wed. I am...

thurs. I am...

fri. I am...

sat. I am...

sun. I am...

Rituals and Daily Gratitude

Rituals are a beautiful way to connect to your inner being throughout life, and they can be powerfully symbolic and open the floodgates to a deeper connection to the Universe within.

The key essence of trying any ritual is to show up with an open heart, an open mind and a willingness to be open to all possibilities.

Rituals can be used to turn positive energy and spark intentions by activating the Law of Attraction and manifesting your deepest desires.

It is important with any ritual practice that you set your intention, visualise that intention, and take actions towards achieving that vision.

Rituals don't just need to be used to manifest your visions (before an event), but can also be very effective to reflect on your progress (after an event).

One of the most powerful ways to reflect is using HER Daily Gratitude Journal to focus on what actions you have completed towards your goals and vision, as well as what other positives are present in your business and life right now.

Unlike many rituals, this exercise is most effective when completed at the end of each day - usually after completing your working day, or just before going to bed, work well.

HER Daily Gratitude Journal

DATE: ....

TODAY I'M GRATEFUL FOR

WHO MADE ME HAPPY TODAY

WHAT MADE ME HAPPY TODAY

WHAT I'VE DONE WELL TODAY

....
....
....
....

MOMENTS I WILL REMEMBER FROM TODAY

THINGS I'VE ACHIEVED TODAY

....
....
....

EVERYDAY I WILL FOCUS ON WHAT I HAVE IN MY LIFE, AND THAT TODAY I DID MY BEST WITH WHAT I HAVE

HER Daily Gratitude Journal

DATE: ....

TODAY I'M GRATEFUL FOR

WHO MADE ME
HAPPY TODAY

WHAT I'VE DONE WELL TODAY

WHAT MADE ME
HAPPY TODAY

MOMENTS I WILL
REMEMBER FROM
TODAY

THINGS I'VE ACHIEVED TODAY

EVERYDAY I WILL FOCUS ON WHAT I HAVE IN MY LIFE, AND THAT TODAY I DID MY BEST WITH WHAT I HAVE

HER Daily Gratitude Journal

DATE: ....

TODAY I'M GRATEFUL FOR

WHO MADE ME HAPPY TODAY

WHAT MADE ME HAPPY TODAY

WHAT I'VE DONE WELL TODAY

MOMENTS I WILL REMEMBER FROM TODAY

THINGS I'VE ACHIEVED TODAY

EVERYDAY I WILL FOCUS ON WHAT I HAVE IN MY LIFE, AND THAT TODAY I DID MY BEST WITH WHAT I HAVE

HER Daily Gratitude Journal

DATE: ....

TODAY I'M GRATEFUL FOR

WHO MADE ME HAPPY TODAY

WHAT MADE ME HAPPY TODAY

WHAT I'VE DONE WELL TODAY

....
....
....
....

MOMENTS I WILL REMEMBER FROM TODAY

THINGS I'VE ACHIEVED TODAY

....
....
....

EVERYDAY I WILL FOCUS ON WHAT I HAVE IN MY LIFE, AND THAT TODAY I DID MY BEST WITH WHAT I HAVE

HER Daily Gratitude Journal

DATE: ....

TODAY I'M GRATEFUL FOR

WHO MADE ME
HAPPY TODAY

WHAT I'VE DONE WELL TODAY

WHAT MADE ME
HAPPY TODAY

THINGS I'VE ACHIEVED TODAY

MOMENTS I WILL
REMEMBER FROM
TODAY

EVERYDAY I WILL FOCUS ON WHAT I HAVE IN MY LIFE, AND THAT TODAY I DID MY BEST WITH WHAT I HAVE

HER Daily Gratitude Journal

DATE: ....

TODAY I'M GRATEFUL FOR

WHO MADE ME HAPPY TODAY

WHAT MADE ME HAPPY TODAY

WHAT I'VE DONE WELL TODAY

MOMENTS I WILL REMEMBER FROM TODAY

THINGS I'VE ACHIEVED TODAY

EVERYDAY I WILL FOCUS ON WHAT I HAVE IN MY LIFE, AND THAT TODAY I DID MY BEST WITH WHAT I HAVE

HER Daily Gratitude Journal

DATE: ....

TODAY I'M GRATEFUL FOR

WHO MADE ME HAPPY TODAY

WHAT MADE ME HAPPY TODAY

WHAT I'VE DONE WELL TODAY

MOMENTS I WILL REMEMBER FROM TODAY

THINGS I'VE ACHIEVED TODAY

EVERYDAY I WILL FOCUS ON WHAT I HAVE IN MY LIFE, AND THAT TODAY I DID MY BEST WITH WHAT I HAVE

HER Daily Gratitude Journal

DATE: ....

TODAY I'M GRATEFUL FOR

WHO MADE ME HAPPY TODAY

WHAT MADE ME HAPPY TODAY

WHAT I'VE DONE WELL TODAY

....
....
....
....

MOMENTS I WILL REMEMBER FROM TODAY

THINGS I'VE ACHIEVED TODAY

....
....
....

EVERYDAY I WILL FOCUS ON WHAT I HAVE IN MY LIFE, AND THAT TODAY I DID MY BEST WITH WHAT I HAVE

HER Daily Gratitude Journal

DATE: ....

TODAY I'M GRATEFUL FOR

WHO MADE ME HAPPY TODAY

WHAT MADE ME HAPPY TODAY

WHAT I'VE DONE WELL TODAY

MOMENTS I WILL REMEMBER FROM TODAY

THINGS I'VE ACHIEVED TODAY

EVERYDAY I WILL FOCUS ON WHAT I HAVE IN MY LIFE, AND THAT TODAY I DID MY BEST WITH WHAT I HAVE

HER Daily Gratitude Journal

DATE: ....

TODAY I'M GRATEFUL FOR

WHO MADE ME HAPPY TODAY

WHAT MADE ME HAPPY TODAY

WHAT I'VE DONE WELL TODAY

....
....
....
....

MOMENTS I WILL REMEMBER FROM TODAY

THINGS I'VE ACHIEVED TODAY

⭐ ....
⭐ ....
⭐ ....

EVERYDAY I WILL FOCUS ON WHAT I HAVE IN MY LIFE, AND THAT TODAY I DID MY BEST WITH WHAT I HAVE

HER Daily Gratitude Journal

DATE: ....

TODAY I'M GRATEFUL FOR

WHO MADE ME HAPPY TODAY

WHAT I'VE DONE WELL TODAY

....
....
....
....

WHAT MADE ME HAPPY TODAY

THINGS I'VE ACHIEVED TODAY

....
....
....

MOMENTS I WILL REMEMBER FROM TODAY

EVERYDAY I WILL FOCUS ON WHAT I HAVE IN MY LIFE, AND THAT TODAY I DID MY BEST WITH WHAT I HAVE

HER Daily Gratitude Journal

DATE: ....

TODAY I'M GRATEFUL FOR

WHO MADE ME HAPPY TODAY

WHAT MADE ME HAPPY TODAY

WHAT I'VE DONE WELL TODAY

....
....
....
....

MOMENTS I WILL REMEMBER FROM TODAY

THINGS I'VE ACHIEVED TODAY

....
....
....

EVERYDAY I WILL FOCUS ON WHAT I HAVE IN MY LIFE, AND THAT TODAY I DID MY BEST WITH WHAT I HAVE

HER Daily Gratitude Journal

DATE: ....

TODAY I'M GRATEFUL FOR

WHO MADE ME HAPPY TODAY

WHAT MADE ME HAPPY TODAY

WHAT I'VE DONE WELL TODAY

....
....
....
....

MOMENTS I WILL REMEMBER FROM TODAY

THINGS I'VE ACHIEVED TODAY

....
....
....

EVERYDAY I WILL FOCUS ON WHAT I HAVE IN MY LIFE, AND THAT TODAY I DID MY BEST WITH WHAT I HAVE

HER Daily Gratitude Journal

DATE: ....

TODAY I'M GRATEFUL FOR

WHO MADE ME HAPPY TODAY

WHAT MADE ME HAPPY TODAY

WHAT I'VE DONE WELL TODAY

MOMENTS I WILL REMEMBER FROM TODAY

THINGS I'VE ACHIEVED TODAY

EVERYDAY I WILL FOCUS ON WHAT I HAVE IN MY LIFE, AND THAT TODAY I DID MY BEST WITH WHAT I HAVE

HER Daily Gratitude Journal

DATE: ....

TODAY I'M GRATEFUL FOR

WHO MADE ME HAPPY TODAY

WHAT MADE ME HAPPY TODAY

WHAT I'VE DONE WELL TODAY

MOMENTS I WILL REMEMBER FROM TODAY

THINGS I'VE ACHIEVED TODAY

EVERYDAY I WILL FOCUS ON WHAT I HAVE IN MY LIFE, AND THAT TODAY I DID MY BEST WITH WHAT I HAVE

HER Daily Gratitude Journal

HER Business Revolution
Because we are all superwomen

DATE: ....

TODAY I'M GRATEFUL FOR

WHO MADE ME HAPPY TODAY

WHAT MADE ME HAPPY TODAY

WHAT I'VE DONE WELL TODAY

....
....
....
....

MOMENTS I WILL REMEMBER FROM TODAY

THINGS I'VE ACHIEVED TODAY

⭐ ....
⭐ ....
⭐ ....

EVERYDAY I WILL FOCUS ON WHAT I HAVE IN MY LIFE, AND THAT TODAY I DID MY BEST WITH WHAT I HAVE

HER Daily Gratitude Journal

DATE: ....

TODAY I'M GRATEFUL FOR

WHO MADE ME HAPPY TODAY

WHAT MADE ME HAPPY TODAY

WHAT I'VE DONE WELL TODAY

MOMENTS I WILL REMEMBER FROM TODAY

THINGS I'VE ACHIEVED TODAY

⭐
⭐
⭐

EVERYDAY I WILL FOCUS ON WHAT I HAVE IN MY LIFE, AND THAT TODAY I DID MY BEST WITH WHAT I HAVE

HER Daily Gratitude Journal

DATE: ....

TODAY I'M GRATEFUL FOR

WHO MADE ME HAPPY TODAY

WHAT MADE ME HAPPY TODAY

WHAT I'VE DONE WELL TODAY

MOMENTS I WILL REMEMBER FROM TODAY

THINGS I'VE ACHIEVED TODAY

EVERYDAY I WILL FOCUS ON WHAT I HAVE IN MY LIFE, AND THAT TODAY I DID MY BEST WITH WHAT I HAVE

HER Daily Gratitude Journal

DATE: ....

TODAY I'M GRATEFUL FOR

WHO MADE ME HAPPY TODAY

WHAT MADE ME HAPPY TODAY

WHAT I'VE DONE WELL TODAY

MOMENTS I WILL REMEMBER FROM TODAY

THINGS I'VE ACHIEVED TODAY

EVERYDAY I WILL FOCUS ON WHAT I HAVE IN MY LIFE, AND THAT TODAY I DID MY BEST WITH WHAT I HAVE

HER Daily Gratitude Journal

DATE: ....

TODAY I'M GRATEFUL FOR

WHO MADE ME HAPPY TODAY

WHAT MADE ME HAPPY TODAY

WHAT I'VE DONE WELL TODAY

....
....
....
....

MOMENTS I WILL REMEMBER FROM TODAY

THINGS I'VE ACHIEVED TODAY

....
....
....

EVERYDAY I WILL FOCUS ON WHAT I HAVE IN MY LIFE, AND THAT TODAY I DID MY BEST WITH WHAT I HAVE

HER Final Thoughts

When we are faced with barriers to our business success, or even a larger crisis that has a bigger impact on our life and business as a whole, it can become quite disheartening and make us want to give up completely.

Our mental health and wellbeing can suffer a lot during these times, however with some support and guidance from this HER Business Planner & Wellbeing Journal I hope that you have found some ways to take steps and actions to face the challenges head on - and rise like a phoenix from the ashes!

As well as this, here are some unique ways HER Business Revolution can help you through this time:

1. Share your posts and offerings - tag people in, share on our social media platforms, add details to our weekly bot messages and monthly newsletters to thousands of women.

2. Offer you our Hostess Opportunity - with more of our networking meetings online for the foreseeable future we need more Hostesses to deal with increasing demand for the support and

training we give at our meetings - you can earn referral commission from any Superwomen Membership Club sign ups from your meetings, as well as gain lots of other opportunities for your business (check out:

www.herbusinessrevolution.biz/business-opportu nity).

3. Become a HER Business Revolution affiliate and share our stuff to help us grow our network of incredible Female Entrepreneurs and Women in Business, which also helps you (plus earn Amazon vouchers as part of our Superwomen Membership Club referral scheme too - www.herbusinessrevolution.biz/superwomen-me mbership-club-referral-programme)

So, if you are not yet a member, and you would like to be part of our "people-focused" supportive culture, and our "revolutionary" mission to see every woman succeed (and achieve true equality to men) in business and in life, then you can find our full set of business trainings; along with expert advice, mentoring, support and promotional opportunities, plus lots more; in our club of talented and ambitious Business Superwomen at:

www.herbusinessrevolution.biz/Superwomen-Members
hip-Club

I wish you all the success in progressing your business journey!

Sending love & good vibes,

Serena xoxo

If you would love to connect with me, and find out more about what's going on at HER Business Revolution, please join our community of supportive and passionate Female Entrepreneurs at:

www.facebook.com/groups/herbusinessrevolution

Printed in Great Britain
by Amazon